The Macmillan Book of
ASTRONOMY

BY ROY A. GALLANT

Illustrations by Ron Miller, Don Dixon, Davis Meltzer, Brian Sullivan

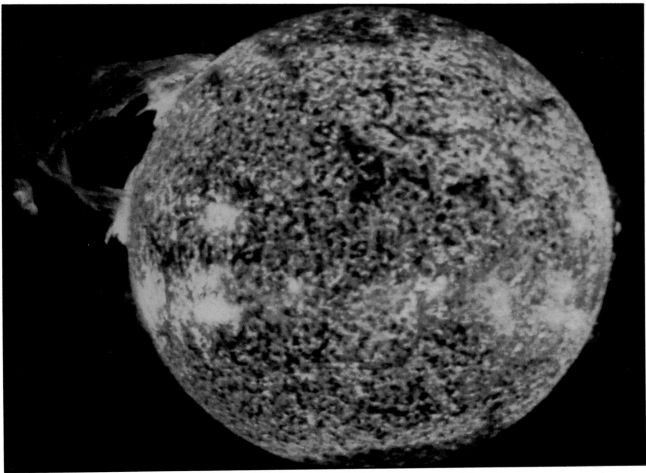

This spectacular prominence on the Sun measures more than 588,000 kilometers across.

Macmillan/McGraw-Hill School Publishing Company
New York Chicago Columbus

ACKNOWLEDGMENTS

I wish to thank Dr. K. L. Franklin, astronomer, friend, colleague, and past Chairman, The American Museum–Hayden Planetarium for reviewing the manuscript for this book. I wish also to thank Rosanna Hansen, my editor, for her thoroughness in maintaining the manuscript at a suitable vocabulary level for the readers of this book, a task of major importance in science publishing. And finally, my thanks to Judith R. Whipple, Publisher of Macmillan's Children's Books for bringing this project and its author together.

For Jason and Travis, stars of a different order.

ILLUSTRATION CREDITS

Cover illustration by Ron Miller
American Museum of Natural History/Courtesy Department Library
    Services: page 41
California Institute of Technology: page 58
NASA (National Aeronautics and Space Administration): title page,
    pages 4, 9, 20, 24, 30, 32-33, 36, 42, 44, 46, 50, 62, 66, 74
Don Dixon: pages 40, 56, 61 bottom, 68-69, 71, 72
Davis Meltzer: pages 6, 13, 38, 72
Ron Miller: pages 10, 14-15, 16, 18, 22-23, 34, 49, 52
Brian Sullivan: pages 26, 27, 28, 29, 55, 61 top, 65

Cover: Neptune as seen from Triton.
The text of this book is set in 12 point Century Expanded.
The illustrations are prepared in watercolor and reproduced in full color.

Text copyright © 1986 by Roy A. Gallant
Illustations copyright © 1986 by **Macmillan Publishing Company**,
    a division of Macmillan, Inc.

Aladdin Books
Macmillan Publishing Company
866 Third Avenue, New York, NY 10022
Collier Macmillan Canada, Inc.

The Macmillan Book of Astronomy is also published in a hardcover edition by
Macmillan Publishing Company.
First Collier/Aladdin edition 1986

For information regarding permission, write to Aladdin Books, **Macmillan Publishing Company,** 866 Third Avenue, New York, NY 10022.

This edition is reprinted by arrangement with
Macmillan Publishing Company.

Macmillan/McGraw-Hill School Division
10 Union Square East
New York, New York 10003

Printed and bound in Mexico.
ISBN 0-02-274941-1

5 6 7 8 9 REY 99 98 97 96 95

CONTENTS

OUR HOME IN SPACE

Imagine that you are a scientist from another planet. Your spaceship has crossed many kilometers of space and finally is nearing Earth.

The picture on the opposite page shows what you would see from a few thousand kilometers away—a sparkling blue planet with featherlike clouds floating in a deep layer of air. So much water covers Earth that it might better be called "the Water Planet." The eight other planets you saw on your way through the Solar System to Earth did not have water, so Earth is special in that way. Through the clouds you can make out reddish-brown and gray shapes of land. There also are two large white patches at opposite sides of Earth, at the poles.

As your spaceship circles Earth and comes closer, you see many silver ribbons of water—Earth's rivers. You also see large green regions of forests, and you can make out many patches that stand out sharply from the mountains, lakes, and other natural features. They are cities, with straight criss-crossing lines, partly hidden by smoke and ash coming from many of their buildings. As your spaceship continues to circle, you pass into Earth's shadow and view its night side. The cities now appear as island clusters of fireflies. You realize that Earth is special in another way—it has many forms of life.

As your spaceship moves out of Earth's shadow and around to the daylight side again, the Sun blazes into view. It is the Sun that gives Earth the energy to keep all its living things healthy, and makes life itself possible. What is the Sun? Is it made of the same matter that makes up Earth? What makes the Sun shine, and how can it be so hot?

Earth rises over the Moon's horizon.

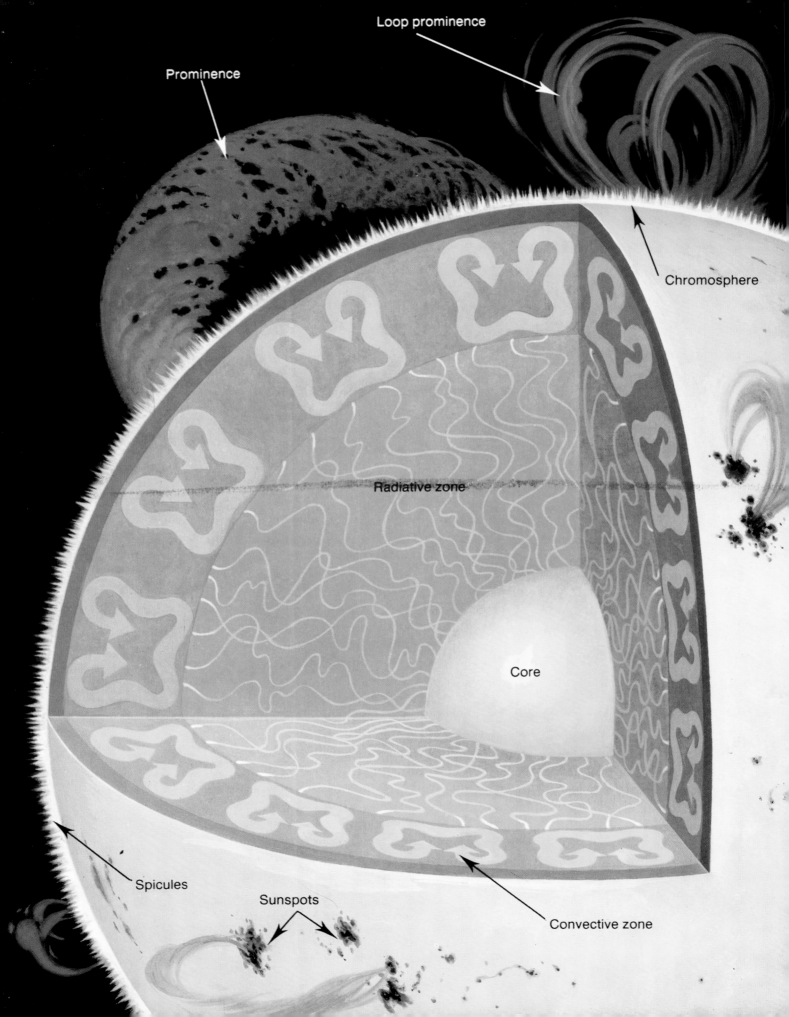

THE SUN:
Our Local Star

The Sun is never at rest. It is always changing. Churning gases hotter than fire boil up to its surface. What is it made of? What makes it shine? Can it keep shining forever?

The Sun is a star. Stars are great balls of hot gases that pour out huge amounts of heat, light, and other energy. Since the Sun is the star nearest our home planet, it is the star we know best. But it is so far away that it would take us more than 17 years to fly there in a jet airplane. The Sun is so large that, if it were hollow, it could hold more than a million Earths. And 100 Earths could be lined up across the middle of the Sun.

Imagine that we could fly to the Sun and journey right down into its center or core. What would we find?

Sunshine at the Core

Years ago, people thought the Sun was a huge ball of fire. Today, we know that cannot be so. Why? Because a lump of coal or piece of wood the size of the Sun would burn for only a few thousand years. Astronomers have good reasons to think that the Sun has been shining for nearly 5 billion years.

The Sun's energy comes, not from fire, but from fusion. Fusion happens when four atoms of a gas called hydrogen combine or fuse to form one atom of helium, another gas. When hydrogen fuses into helium, lots of energy is given off. There is so much fusion energy from the Sun that we feel the Sun's heat on Earth—150 million kilometers or 93 million miles away.

In this painting of the Sun's core, arrows show the way hot gases in the convection zone of the Sun rise and fall.

Fusion occurs only when hydrogen becomes very hot. And the core of the Sun *is* very hot. Astronomers think that the core temperature of the Sun is 15 million kelvins. (Kelvins are used to measure very high and very low temperatures. Room temperature in kelvin degrees is about 300, which is 68°F on your living room thermometer.) In the next chapter, you will learn how the Sun grew so hot.

The Sun's core is very tightly packed with hydrogen and helium. It is so tightly packed that the energy of fusion takes 50 million years to work its way up to the Sun's surface. But that energy then crosses the great distance to Earth in only 8 minutes, because it travels at the speed of light (300,000 kilometers or 186,000 miles per second). Much of the energy is light. Some is heat, some radio waves, some X-ray and some is the energy that gives you sunburn on the beach.

The Sun's Soft "Surface"

Moving outward from the core, we would come to the surface of the sun, a boiling sea of hot gases called the photosphere or "light sphere." The temperature of this gas layer is much lower—only 6,000 kelvins.

Hot swelling mountains of gas called granules keep the photosphere churning. Dark patches called sunspots come and go among the granules. Though they are called "spots," a typical sunspot is about the size of Earth. They appear dark because their gases are cooler than the hotter gases around them. The Sun breaks out in sunspots about every 11 years. The next active sunspot period will be 1991–1992.

In 1612, the Italian astronomer Galileo was the first to study sunspots through a telescope. By following their motion across the Sun, he saw that the Sun rotates or spins around once every 27 days. Galileo became blind because he looked straight into the Sun. NEVER LOOK STRAIGHT AT THE SUN, NOT EVEN FOR A FEW SECONDS. IT WILL DAMAGE YOUR EYES.

Storms in the Chromosphere

Above the Sun's surface is the chromosphere or "color sphere." During an eclipse of the Sun, it appears as a thin pinkish rim around the hidden Sun. The chromosphere is a raging layer of gases about 2,500 kilometers deep. Huge tongues of hot gas called spicules or "little spikes" leap 10,000 kilometers (6,200 miles) high. They shoot up from huge cells of gas, which measure some 30,000 kilometers (18,650 miles) across.

Often, great loops of hot gases break through the chromosphere.

They arch to heights of 100,000 kilometers (62,000 miles) or more. The chromosphere also lights up with violent explosions called flares. They can be several thousand kilometers wide and last from a few minutes to an hour. A single flare may give off the energy of 10 million hydrogen bombs! When the Sun is especially active, flares explode almost every hour and cast off streams of pieces of atoms. The streams race across space and batter Earth's upper atmosphere, causing the Northern Lights.

Journey Outward Through the Corona

During an eclipse, when the Moon blocks the Sun's light, we can photograph the Sun's feathery outer atmosphere. It is called the corona, which means "crown." The corona stretches far outward from the chromosphere. The shape of the corona changes. Sometimes we see it shrunken, other times swollen. Sometimes hot streams of pieces of atoms are hurled outward and across the Solar System. These streams are called the solar wind.

The Sun has been shining for 5 billion years, and astronomers tell us that the Sun will keep shining for another 5 billion years. The Sun can shine for so long because it fuses only a little hydrogen as it produces large amounts of energy. It is a good thing that the Sun has such a long, bright future, because all life on Earth depends on the Sun. Its energy keeps us from freezing, provides us with the food we eat, and causes the wind and all our weather.

The colors in this photo of the corona, the Sun's outer atmosphere, were made brighter by a computer. White represents the highest intensity of light and violet the lowest intensity.

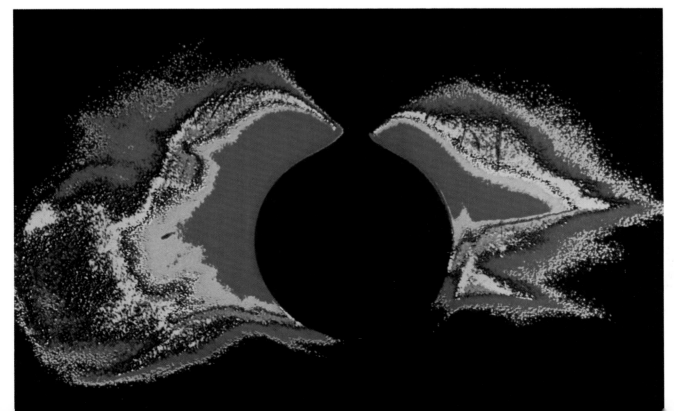

THE SOLAR SYSTEM: The Beginning

The Sun is one of trillions of stars in the Universe. Compared with most other stars, the Sun is not especially hot or large. But to us it is a very special star. It pours forth heat and light that make Earth a home for more than 2 million different kinds of plants and animals.

Like all other stars, the Sun has not always been shining. And one day it must go out, but that day will not come for many, many millions of years. The Sun began nearly 5 billion years ago as a great cloud of hydrogen gas. It is only one of some 500 billion stars collected in a huge spinning wheel of stars, gas, and space "dust" called a galaxy. Our home galaxy is named the Milky Way, and the Sun is located out toward its edge.

Stardust for the Sun

Many other stars of the Milky Way formed long before the Sun did. Some of those stars were giants with so much matter, or mass, packed into them that they exploded. Later we will find out why stars with lots of mass explode. The cloud of matter that was to become the Sun was made mostly of hydrogen along with some helium. But the young Sun-cloud also had many atoms much heavier than hydrogen and helium. Those heavier atoms were thrown off by superstars that ended their lives in giant explosions.

After it was formed, the young Sun-cloud shrank. Its matter began to tumble in toward the center. Gravity, the force that pulls you down to the ground, caused the Sun-cloud's matter to tumble toward the center. The cloud was some 30 billion kilometers (20

The sizes of the planets and their moons are shown to scale against the background of the Sun.

billion miles) across and had about twice as much matter as the Sun has today. Gravity kept pulling the matter in the Sun-cloud more and more tightly together. So the cloud gradually closed in on itself. As it closed in, it grew very hot in the center. It then began to spin and flatten until eventually it hurled off a huge spinning wheel of gas and dust. About 90 percent of the cloud-matter formed a ball at the center of the wheel. It was this tightly packed ball of hot and glowing matter that eventually became our Sun.

The Planets Form

The huge spinning wheel of leftover matter stretched out far from the spinning Sun. Tiny dust grains within the wheel bumped into each other and began clumping together. Larger clumps attracted smaller clumps that stuck together. Eventually the wheel had many billions of solid objects from a few centimeters to many meters in size. Clumps with lots of mass swept up less massive clumps and so grew larger. Astronomers now think that the planets were formed by this clumping process. Some of the solid clumps were made of ice, others of rocky matter. Still others had lots of heavier matter such as iron. While the planets were forming this way, so were their moons. Far out near the edge of the young Solar System lots of icy matter mixed with dust was left over and never swept up into planets or moons. This material became the Solar System's comets.

The Sun Begins to Shine

At first the young Sun was a cool ball of gas that kept drawing matter from the wheel into itself. But farther out in the wheel, out near Jupiter and beyond, the pull of the Sun's gravity was weaker. More matter seems to have been left over out here than in closer to the Sun where Earth is. This may help explain why the inner planets of our Solar System (Mercury, Venus, Earth, and Mars) are smaller than the outer giant planets (Jupiter, Saturn, Uranus, and Neptune). Unlike the smaller inner planets, the giant outer planets attracted and held lots of gases and solid matter of the Sun-cloud.

As the young Sun kept pulling nearby matter into itself, its core grew hotter and hotter. This heating was caused by the tight packing of matter down into the core region. Soon the Sun heated up enough to glow a cherry red. All around our young Sun was a dense fog of leftover gas and dust grains through which the newly formed planets moved. Space in the Solar System at this time must have been very foggy. After about 100 million years, the Sun became hot enough to shine with a yellowish-white light. When the Sun began to fuse hydrogen into helium, the young star sent huge bursts of light, heat, and other energy sweeping through the Solar System. These solar gales cleared away the foggy gas and dust left in the wheel. Space between the planets then became clear, as it is today.

No one can say for certain that the Sun and its family of planets formed in exactly that way. But all the evidence points to some such process. Today the Solar System is an orderly family with our huge star, the Sun, at its center. Surrounding the star are nine known planets: Mercury (the nearest), Venus, Earth, Mars, Jupiter (the largest), Saturn, Uranus, Neptune, and Pluto (the most distant). Each revolves around the Sun at its own special speed—Mercury the fastest, Pluto the slowest. Each planet also rotates or spins on its axis at its own special speed. It takes Earth 24 hours to make one complete rotation, and 365¼ days to revolve once around the Sun. The other planets have different lengths of days and years.

Many of the planets have moons (bodies that revolve around them). We have counted about 50 moons in the Solar System so far. There are also thousands of boulders and mountain-size rocks called asteroids. And there are billions of meteroids and comets. All of the Solar System—planets, moons, asteroids, meteoroids, and comets—is held in place by the force that gave birth to it all—the force of gravity.

This three-stage diagram shows how the Solar System probably was formed out of a giant cloud of gas and dust almost five billion years ago.

Earliest Stage

Most Recent Stage

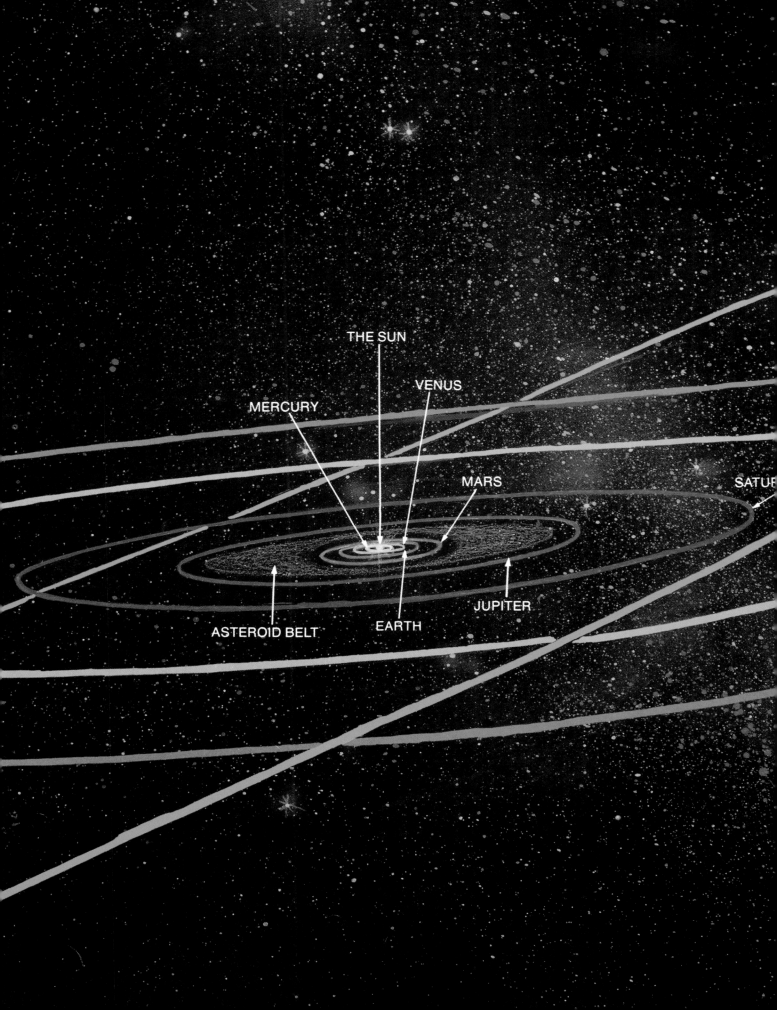

PLUTO

URANUS

NEPTUNE

The planets are shown in their orbits around the Sun. Compare the distances of the planets from the Sun and from each other.

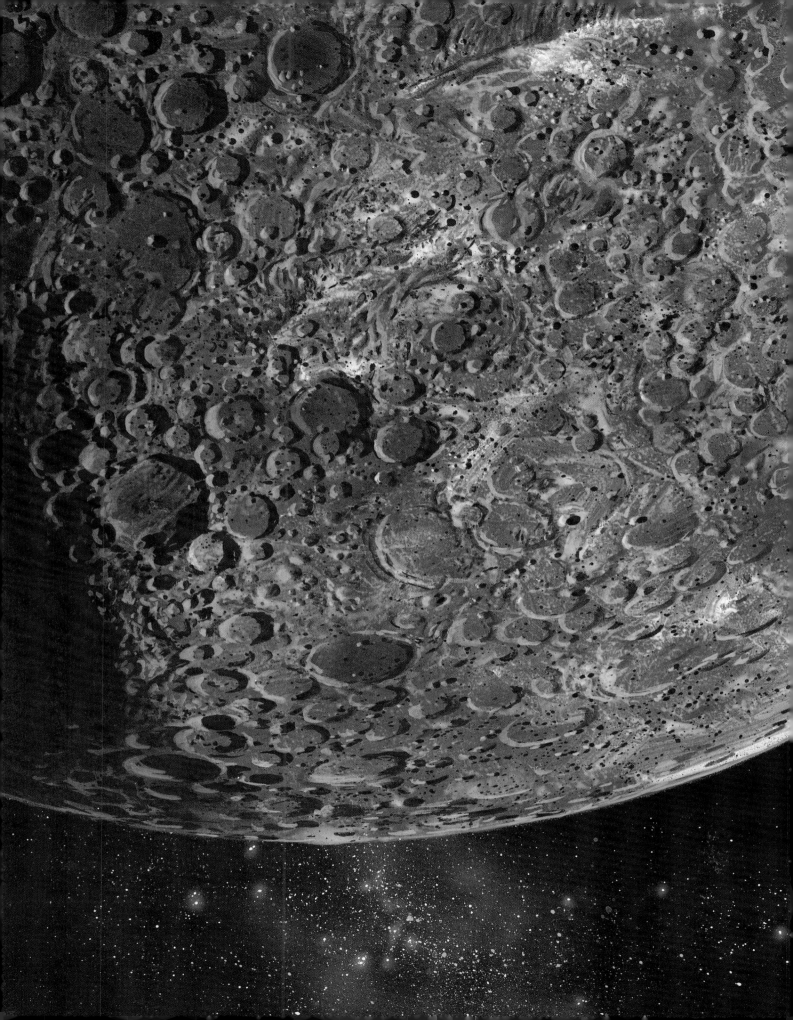

MERCURY: A Battered World

In the spring of 1974 a small spacecraft named *Mariner 10* gave us our first close-up view of the Sun's nearest planet, swift little Mercury. Exciting photos showed that the planet has many craters, mountains, and valleys, like those on the Moon. The photos were taken from a distance of only 705 kilometers (438 miles). That is about the distance of Portland, Maine from New York City. Mariner also told us that Mercury, like Earth, acts like a magnet and has a magnetic field. You may have seen pictures in your science books showing a magnetic field looping around a bar magnet. Mercury's magnetic field protects the planet from damaging pieces of matter hurled out by the Sun.

Of all the planets, Mercury circles the Sun fastest. It does one orbit every 88 days. Mercury and the other planets are held in orbit around the Sun by the Sun's gravity. Because Mercury is so close to the blindingly bright Sun, the planet is very hard to study through telescopes. It wasn't until *Mariner 10* that we learned about Mercury's surface features.

Mercury does not have a blanket of air to keep the sunlit side from heating up or the shadow side from cooling. Because Mercury is so close to the Sun, its sunlit face heats up to 427°C, twice as hot as an oven baking a cake. And the shadow side of the planet dips to −183°C. Mercury's long day—nearly three Earth months long—allows plenty of time for its surface rocks to heat up between sunrise and sunset, and to cool off in its equally long night.

This painting of the heavily cratered surface of Mercury shows how the planet looked from the *Mariner 10* spacecraft.

Rock Bombs from Space

Mercury is less than half Earth's size. It has thousands of craters. Some are 100 meters (330 feet) or less across, while others are deep bowls as wide as Texas. More than 100 of its craters have white, powderlike rays. It is as if the craters were formed by giant bags of flour smashing into the planet. Some of these splashed-out rays are 400 kilometers (250 miles) long. One of the brightest ray craters is named Kuiper, after the U.S. astronomer Gerard P. Kuiper. Many of Mercury's craters are named to honor writers, musicians, and artists. The craters were formed early in the history of the Solar System when all the planets were bombed by chunks of rock and metal like those making up the asteroids today. Because Mercury is without air or water, the craters have not been worn away by rain and wind. So the planet's face is as sharp and fresh as it was millions of years ago.

Mercury has a very interesting region called the Caloris Basin, meaning "hot basin." Larger than all of New England, it has a rim of mountains about 2 kilometers (1¼ miles) high. The basin itself has rugged mountains and a curved chain of wavy ridges and scattered craters. A giant asteroid 75 kilometers (45 miles) across may have smashed into Mercury and made the Caloris Basin. The great shock of the crash threw up a jumble of features called Mercury's "peculiar terrain" on the *opposite* side. The peculiar terrain looks like the face of a prune with mountain ridges up to 2 kilometers (1¼ miles) high.

Mercury also has steep slopes called scarps. Up to 3 kilometers (2 miles) high, some zigzag across the planet for a few hundred kilometers. The scarps formed after the craters. In its youth Mercury was a hot ball of melted rock and metal. As it slowly cooled over many millions of years, the planet may have shrunk a bit and wrinkled, forming the scarps. The scarps are named after famous ships of discovery, such as the *Victoria, Santa Maria,* and *Discovery.*

Mercury has a rock crust made of the same kind of rock found on Earth. Beneath the crust is a thicker mantle layer of the same material. The planet's core may be a ball of hot metal—nickel and iron—about the size of the Moon.

A long ledge, called a scarp, cuts through one of Mercury's many craters. This means that the crater was formed before the scarp.

VENUS: The Hottest Planet

The second planet out from the Sun is Venus. Venus is one of the best explored planets beyond Earth. The *Mariner 10* spacecraft, which photographed Mercury, also photographed Venus. In addition to Mariner, 16 other spacecraft have explored Venus—12 Soviet spacecraft and 4 American. Astronomers once thought of Venus as a "twin" planet of Earth. But Venus has turned out to be a strange twin.

An Atmosphere of Acid Clouds

Venus is always hidden beneath deep clouds. They rise to about 70 kilometers (45 miles) above the planet's surface. Strong winds about 350 kilometers an hour (220 miles an hour) keep Venus's yellowish clouds in motion. Unlike Earth's clouds of tiny drops of water, Venus's clouds have a deadly acid—sulfuric acid. The top cloud layers are very cold at −45°C. But down near the surface they heat up.

Venus's heavy air is about 97 percent carbon dioxide. That is the poisonous gas we breathe out. The other 3 percent of Venus's air is nitrogen. The planet's clouds begin about 30 kilometers (20 miles) above the surface. Below that the air is clear of clouds. But the air is so dense that anything more than 100 meters away would look blurred. It would be almost like looking down through water at the lake bottom. Venus's air is a never-ending storm, always booming with thunder and torn by about 25 lightning flashes every second.

The yellow clouds that mask Venus change their patterns over the years.

Spacecraft have mapped the planet and photographed the surface. But the air near the surface is so dense and so hot that the longest any of the craft could operate was less than 2 hours. The air pressure at Venus's surface is 90 times that on Earth, and the temperature is 460°C. That is hot enough to melt lead. Venus's surface winds are gentle, only about 4 kilometers (2½ miles) an hour. But the air is so dense that the winds are more like a current of river water than a breeze.

A Hothouse Planet with a Red Sky

Venus's dense air would hold many surprises for an Earth visitor. For one, the sky would appear a deep red instead of blue. Why? Because the dense air scatters blue light so widely that we wouldn't see much blue. Instead our vision would be much better in the red light at the opposite end of the color spectrum. The landscape would also seem bent. This is because the dense air makes light follow a bent path instead of a straight path. It would be as if we were standing in the middle of a huge soup bowl and looking up toward the rim. If we could see the sun through the clouds, we would see it as a stretched-out blob of color flattened along the horizon.

Why is Venus hotter than Mercury? After all, Venus is farther away from the Sun. The answer is so much carbon dioxide in Venus's air. The Sun's rays go down through Venus's air and heat the surface rocks. But the carbon dioxide acts as a blanket that traps the heat

given off by Venus's surface. Scientists call this the greenhouse effect because the Sun's heat is trapped as it is in a greenhouse on Earth.

Venus is an eerie world with active volcanoes and a red sky slashed by 25 lightning bolts every second.

Volcanoes, Mountains, and Craters on Venus

By 1980 scientists had mapped nearly all of Venus's surface. A little more than half of Venus's surface is gently rolling flat land. There are few deep basins like Earth's ocean basins. Venus has many craters, but they have been worn down by weather. The American spacecraft *Pioneer Venus 1* found some craters more than 75 kilometers (45 miles) wide. There also are two continent-size highland areas. Venus's highest mountain is named Maxwell Montes. It stretches up 30,300 meters (100,000 feet) and appears to have a big volcanic crater.

Venus has one of the largest canyons in the Solar System. It is nearly four times longer than the Grand Canyon and twice as deep. This is not a canyon scooped out by water. More likely it was made when Venus's rock crust split open long ago. It may be the scene of huge lava flows today, and the canyon may be shaken by Venus-quakes from time to time.

Venus rotates, or turns on its axis, backward. This means a person on Venus would see the Sun rise in the west and set in the east, opposite what we see from Earth. From one sunrise to the next on Venus takes 117 Earth days. Venus seems to have a rock crust of granite, beneath which is a much thicker layer of volcanic rock (basalt). The core of the planet may be a ball of nickel-iron.

23

EARTH: The Watery Planet

More than 4 billion years ago, young Earth became a ball of molten rock and metal. At least, that is what scientists think happened. While the lighter rock material floated up toward the surface, the heavier metals sank into the core region. That seems to be how Earth got its crust of lightweight rocky matter and a core of iron and nickel.

Over millions of years the planet cooled and formed a solid rock crust. The average depth of the crust is about 20 kilometers (12 miles). Sometimes hot rock beneath welled up through large cracks in the crust and flowed over parts of the surface. Sometimes hot rock called lava spurted out of volcanoes. Gases bubbling out of the lava collected as an atmosphere. Some of that gas was water in the form of vapor. As it rose high into the air it cooled, condensed, and fell as rain. It rained for many centuries and the water collected in pools which flowed as rivers. The rivers then drained into deep basins that became our planet's first oceans. Eventually Earth's dense clouds thinned, allowing the Sun to shine through on its third most distant planet, a world of jagged rock and sparkling water.

The Continents Form

The continents we know today began some 220 million years ago as a single supercontinent called Pangaea. By 135 million years ago, Pangaea had broken in two and drifted apart into a northern half called Laurasia and a southern half called Gondwana. By 65 million years ago these two huge land masses also had split in two. The pieces drifted toward the positions of the continents we know today.

A view from space would show Earth's blue oceans and gently swirling white clouds.

As it orbits the Sun, Earth spins on its axis. The part of Earth that is tilted toward the Sun has the summer season.

The sea floor and continents that form Earth's crust are rooted in denser rock that forms the mantle layer. Like Mercury's and Venus's, Earth's rock crust was long ago battered by asteroid impacts that left many craters. Today we know of nearly 80 large craters. But there must have been many thousands more that have been erased by erosion and the passage of glaciers. Those remaining today range in size from less than 100 meters (330 feet) to more than 100 kilometers (62 miles) across.

The mantle is some 2,900 kilometers (1,800 miles) deep. Parts of the mantle are so hot that it is molten. Earth's core has a liquid outer layer surrounding a solid inner ball about 2,600 kilometers (1,615 miles) across. The core is mostly iron with some nickel. The temperature in the core may reach 4,000°C and the pressure there may be more than 3 million times that of the air we breathe.

Life on Earth

Earth is the only planet we know of where life exists. How Earth life first arose is one of the most exciting questions we can ask about our home planet. Most scientists think that some 3.5 billion years ago life formed out of certain chemicals in the water. Tiny living things called bacteria, and other tiny plantlike organisms, began to grow in the seas. Over millions of years some of these organisms evolved into green plants. These plants used water, carbon dioxide, and the energy of sunlight to make their own food, as plants still do. During this process they gave off oxygen, which added to Earth's air and changed it in an important way. The new supply of oxygen made it possible for other living organisms to evolve.

During a total solar eclipse, the Moon moves between the Sun and Earth. The Moon then blocks the Sun's light from shining on a small part of Earth.

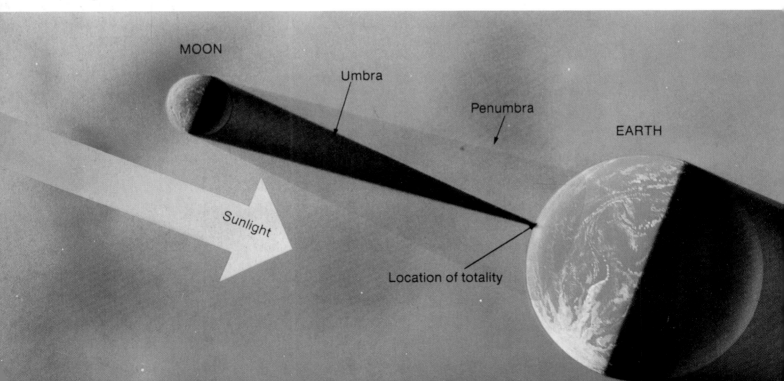

MOON

Umbra

Penumbra

EARTH

Sunlight

Location of totality

FALL

WINTER

SUMMER

SPRING

As hundreds of millions of years passed, plants took up life on land. So did fishlike animals that lived in the seas during the Age of Fishes some 395 to 345 million years ago. Later, during the Age of Reptiles some 225 to 65 million years ago, those "terrible lizards," the dinosaurs, ruled Earth for more than 100 million years. After the passing of the dinosaurs came the Age of Mammals, which came to include humans.

In the geography of the Solar System, Earth is in a special place well suited for life. To be so well off, a planet must be within a certain distance of its local star. If the planet is too close to its local star— like Mercury—it will be too hot for life-giving molecules to form. If it is too far away—like Pluto—it will be too cold for those molecules to join and too cold for liquid water to exist.

Earth's Ocean of Air

We live at the bottom of an ocean of air. The air is 78 percent nitrogen, 21 percent oxygen, and 1 percent carbon dioxide, water vapor, ozone, neon, argon, and other gases. And there is lots of dust mixed in. We can think of Earth's atmosphere as having five layers. The layers are shown on the diagram on this page.

Most of our weather takes place in the troposphere, which extends up about 10 kilometers from Earth's surface. Four more layers of air in the Earth's atmosphere are above the troposphere.

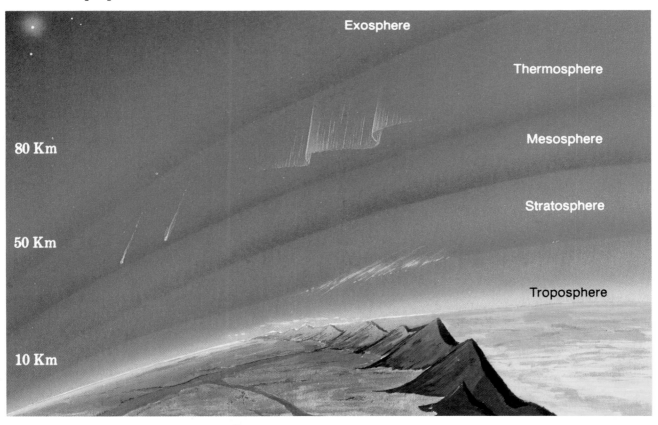

Exosphere

Thermosphere

Mesosphere

Stratosphere

Troposphere

80 Km

50 Km

10 Km

Earth Is a Magnet

Earth acts like a magnet. Like any magnet, our planet has a magnetic field that we can detect with a compass. The field protects us from the dangerous solar wind. Two doughnut-shaped belts of the magnetic field enclose Earth and trap radiation particles of the solar wind. The belts are called the Van Allen radiation belts. When the radiation particles are hurled into Earth's upper air, we see colorful displays of Northern Lights.

Earth revolves around, or circles, the Sun once every 365 days, which we call a year. As it does, it also rotates on its axis once every 24 hours. It is night on Earth when we are on the side of Earth in shadow, or facing away from the Sun. When Earth's rotation brings us out of shadow and back into Sunlight again, it is daytime. Earth's axis is not pointed straight up and down in space but is tilted over, as shown in the diagram on page 27. This tilt gives us the seasons as Earth revolves about the Sun. When the side we live on is tilted down toward the Sun, we have summer because we receive lots of the Sun's heat. Six months later our part of Earth is tilted up away from the Sun and it is winter because we then receive less of the Sun's heat.

Earth's magnetic field protects us from harmful particles of radiation from the Sun. Some of these particles are trapped in two doughnut-shaped regions called the Van Allen belts.

On July 20, 1969, Neil Armstrong, an astronaut,
became the first human to set foot on the Moon.

THE MOON: Our Rocky Neighbor

Earth has one natural satellite, the Moon. It is an airless little world less than one-fourth the size of Earth. The Moon orbits our planet once every 27.3 days at a distance of 380,000 kilometers (240,000 miles) and always shows us the same side.

The Moon's gravity causes ocean tides on Earth. (The Sun does, too, but with less strength.) The Moon raises one large bulge of ocean water and holds the bulge in place as Earth rotates beneath it. In addition to the tidal bulge on the side of Earth facing the Moon, there is a second tidal bulge on the opposite side of Earth. The twin bulges cause most places on Earth to have two high and two low tides each day—a high tide once every 12 hours and 25 minutes followed by a low tide.

The Moon most likely was formed about the same time as Earth and out of much the same solar-wheel material. But the Moon picked up less iron and, therefore, is only 60 percent as dense as Earth.

Like Mercury, the Moon was bombarded by asteroids and so has a heavily cratered surface. Some craters, such as Copernicus, measure 90 kilometers (55 miles) from rim to rim. Some have central peaks and circular mountain walls about 6 kilometers (4 miles) high. Because the Moon lacks air, it is a hot and cold little world, like Mercury. The lunar high-noon temperature reaches 134°C. On the Moon's night side the temperature drops to about −170°C.

At some time in its history, the Moon heated up and melted. The surface rock later hardened, and then molten rock below welled up through cracks in the surface, flooding huge areas. Today we see these areas of solid lava as the Moon's "seas," or maria. Some of the maria are 1,000 kilometers (620 miles) across. Scientists now think that the maria formed about 3 million years ago.

American astronauts first landed on the Moon on July 20, 1969. They returned to Earth on July 24 carrying with them a precious

cargo of Moon rocks. In all, there were six Apollo landings on the Moon, the last one in 1972. They made the Moon our best known, as well as nearest, neighbor in space.

Astronaut Harrison Schmitt has left his lunar rover to gather Moon rocks. One rock, named Split-Rock, is the enormous boulder shown.

MARS: The Red Planet

Mars is the fourth planet from the sun. Until about 20 years ago it was a mysterious reddish world. Our exploration of Mars began with the *Mariner 4* fly-by in 1965. That spacecraft sent back the first close-up photographs of the Red Planet. Then came the two Viking flights that landed on Mars in the summer of 1976. In August, 1978, one of the Viking craft sent back pictures showing what may be a towering column of steam gushing from a geyser or small active volcano. The column rose more than 300 meters (1,000 feet) higher than New York City's Empire State Building. If the cloud turns out to be steam, we will have to change our idea of Mars as a geologically dead world. Since the first Mariner mission we have learned many details about the Martian surface. We also have unraveled some of the puzzles of the planet's past.

A Planet of Wind and Rust

Mars is a little more than half Earth's size and takes nearly twice as long to orbit the Sun. But a day on Mars is nearly the same as an Earth day. The surface rocks on Mars are much like ours.

The planet's soil is mostly the elements silicon and oxygen mixed with metals including iron and magnesium. The soil has a lot of iron oxide (rust) that gives Mars its reddish color. Huge clouds of red dust

Mars's red surface is seen from its moon Deimos, which orbits Mars from about 23,000 kilometers away.

A Martian sunset: the glow of the Sun on the horizon has been enlarged by a computer. Mars's rocky surface appears in the foreground.

and sand are swept up by fierce summer winds in Mars's southern region. These raging dust storms sometimes cover Mars's surface for weeks and months. Thousands of Martian craters, large and small, are visible but are worn down by the sandblasting of the dust storms.

Mars also has many channels that snake over its surface for distances up to 1,600 kilometers (1,000 miles). Some are 10 kilometers (6 miles) deep and 200 kilometers (125 miles) wide. Smaller channels lead into the large ones. Some of these channels may have been carved out by the march of glaciers long ago. Others look as though they were cut by great rivers that dried up long ago.

A broad dome about 5,000 kilometers (3,100 miles) across rises 7 kilometers (4 miles) above Mars's surface along the equator. Called Tharsis, it has four huge ancient volcanoes 27 kilometers (17 miles) high. That is more than twice as high as Earth's highest mountain, Mount Everest. The largest of the four is named Olympus Mons.

Tharsis's eastern edge is cut by a string of canyons called Valles Marineris. In places these canyons are four times deeper than the Grand Canyon and as long as the United States. The Valles Marineris canyons seem to be giant rifts, or gouges in the crust formed by Marsquakes that split the crust long ago.

The most spectacular feature in Mars's southern region is a huge basin some 4 kilometers (2 miles) deep. It is large enough for Alaska to fit inside with room to spare. The basin probably was blasted out by collision with a giant asteroid.

Mars's Air and Polar Caps

Like Earth, Mars long ago collected an atmosphere as gases bubbled out of its molten rock when the planet was young. But Mars's weak gravity let most of those gases escape to space. Today the planet's air is mostly carbon dioxide and the gas argon along with some ozone. There is very little water vapor. Mars's air is so thin that atmospheric pressure at the surface is too low to keep animals alive.

The temperature at the planet's surface climbs to a high of about 25°C at the equator at noon. At the north and south poles, which are covered with ice, it plunges to a low of −123°C. The polar ice is mostly "dry ice" or carbon dioxide, with just a little water ice mixed in. Mars has so little water, in fact, that if you brought it all together, it would form only a small pond.

Potato Moons

The two moons of Mars were discovered in 1877. They are tiny airless and cratered objects that look like battered baked potatoes. They were named Phobos and Deimos after the two sons of the war god and mean "fear" and "terror." Deimos is about 15 kilometers (9 miles) long, Phobos nearly twice that size.

Phobos looks about one third the size of Earth's moon in the night sky of Mars. Deimos appears only as a bright star. The two moons cross the Martian sky in opposite directions. Phobos orbits Mars faster than Mars rotates, while Deimos (like our Moon) orbits slower than Mars rotates.

Life on Mars?

Scientists hoped that the Viking project would answer an old question. Is there life on Mars? With so little water or air on Mars, scientists did not expect to find advanced plants or animals. But they hoped to find simple kinds of life: bacteria or germs.

The Viking craft picked up and examined samples of Martian soil. But no signs of life appeared, as you would find in Earth's soil. Still, nobody is sure that life *doesn't* exist on Mars. The Viking project could study only a few handfuls of soil. Maybe deep underground there is enough water to support life. Or perhaps Mars has forms of life we have not recognized.

ASTEROIDS AND METEOROIDS: Space's Bits and Pieces

In that wide belt of space between Mars and Jupiter are thousands upon thousands of tumbling chunks of rock and metal called the asteroids. They also are called the "minor planets" and "planetoids." Ceres, the largest, is a moonlike globe about 1,000 kilometers (620 miles) across. Others are pear-shaped or odd lumps of rock shattered as the asteroids keep smashing into each other.

A Broken Planet?

Where did the asteroids come from—dumbbell-shaped Hektor; pale Eros that tumbles along end-over-end; and dark, ball-shaped Pallas marked with craters? Years ago astronomers suspected that a planet about the size of Mars once orbited the Sun in the middle of what is now the asteroid belt. Is it possible, they wondered, that Jupiter's powerful gravity gradually pulled the planet closer and closer? If so, eventually the planet would be pulled so close to Jupiter that it would be shattered to bits. Could that be how the asteroids were formed?

One thing that made this idea attractive was that some of the asteroids are all metal, others part metal and part rock, and still others all rock. A shattered planet with a metal core would leave just such a collection of rubble—chunks of metal from the planet's core, part-metal and part-rock pieces from the mantle, and lumps of rock from the crust.

Billions of asteroids, varying in size from a freight car to a mountain, orbit between Mars and Jupiter.

As attractive as this idea was, it has been given up. Most astronomers now think that the asteroids are bits and pieces of matter left over from the time the planets were formed out of the great Sun-cloud of matter. Jupiter's powerful gravity most likely kept a planet from forming nearby and so the asteroids came to be.

Earth-Grazers

Most of the asteroids stay in their wide racetrack-shaped orbits between Mars and Jupiter. But some have long stretched-out orbits that bring them close to Earth now and then. So they are called Earth-grazers.

THIS ASTEROID	COMES THIS CLOSE TO EARTH
Eros	23,000,000 km
Apollo	4,000,000 km
Adonis	2,145,000 km
Hermes	770,000 km

Hermes, the closest Earth-grazer, has zoomed past us, at least once, at a distance only twice that of the Moon. If an asteroid only a few kilometers across smashed into us it would explode and leave a hole as large as Chicago and hundreds of meters deep. Asteroids have smashed into Earth in the past and probably will in the future. But Earth gets only one direct hit every 250,000 years or so.

An asteroid is maneuvered into lunar orbit in this painting.

40

Meteoroids, Meteors, and Meteorites

There are many collisions among the asteroids. As some crash into each other they shatter into bits and pieces called meteoroids. The collisions send the meteoroids flying off in all directions across the Solar System. Some zoom into Earth's atmosphere at speeds of 15 to 72 kilometers (9 to 45 miles) a second. Friction with the atmosphere makes the meteoroids so hot that they burn up in a fiery streak of light called a meteor. Away from city lights on a clear night you can see about 5 meteors an hour after midnight. Years ago people thought meteors were stars that fell out of the sky, so they called them "falling stars" and "shooting stars." When a meteoroid survives its hot journey through Earth's air and falls to the ground, it is called a meteorite.

The largest known meteorite fell on Namibia and weighs 60 tons. The largest meteorite ever dug up is the Ahnighito meteorite, weighing 34 tons. It was shipped from Greenland to New York City by Admiral Peary and today is on display at The American Museum of Natural History in New York City. We know of about 80 large meteorite craters on Earth, but probably there are many more.

The tiniest meteorites are called micrometeorites. You can think of them as dust grains from space. About 10 tons of this material rain down on Earth every day. Sporadic meteors fall to Earth from every direction and probably come from the asteroid belt. But there also are shower meteors, which are the remains of broken comets. We will say more about shower meteors when we describe comets (on page 59).

We can think of the sporadic meteorites as tiny asteroids. In keeping with the makeup of the asteroids, we find three major kinds of meteorites: Stony meteorites are mostly rock with small amounts of iron and nickel. Almost 90 percent of all meteorites are stony. Iron meteorites are part iron and part nickel. Stony-iron meteorites are about half rock and half iron-nickel.

The Ahnighito meteorite was found in Greenland and taken to The American Museum of Natural History in New York City.

41

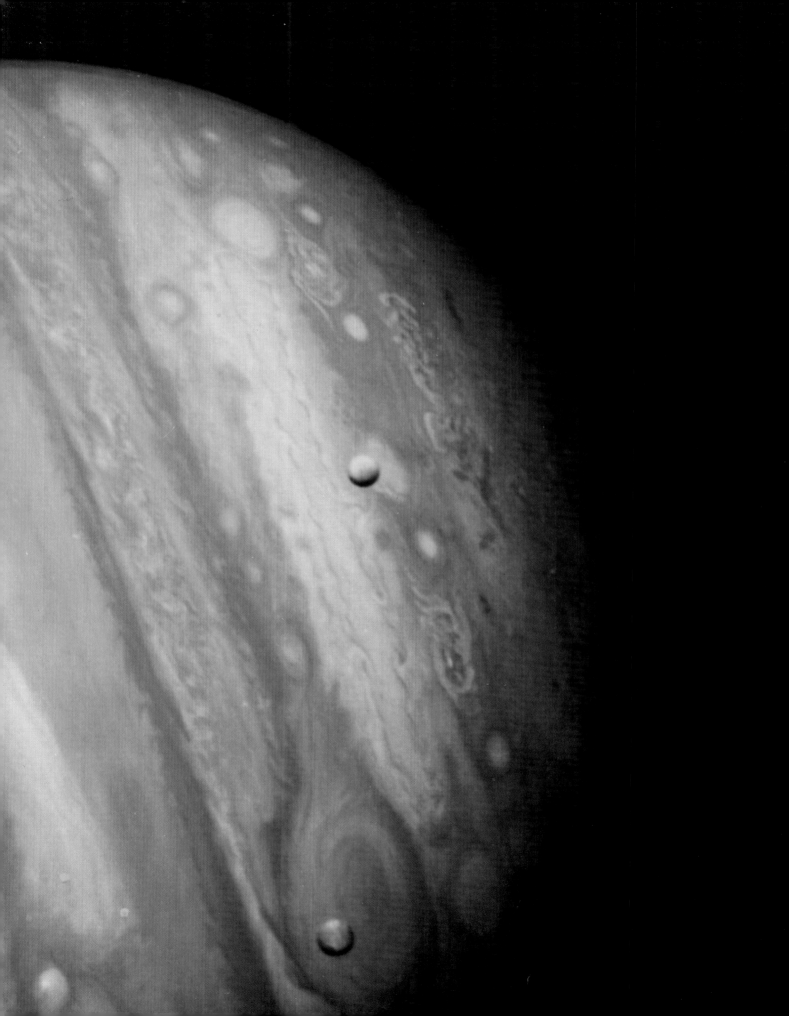

JUPITER: King of the Planets

Jupiter, the largest planet, is second only to the Sun in size. It has more than two-thirds of the Solar System's matter, not counting the Sun. Thirteen hundred Earths could fit inside Jupiter, and 11 Earths could line up across its equator. Jupiter is the first of the four giant planets. The other three are Saturn, Uranus, and Neptune. Just as the inner "terrestrial" planets—Mercury, Venus, Earth, and Mars—have certain things in common, so do the four giants.

Exploring Jupiter

The two Voyager spacecraft, launched in August and September of 1977, taught us a great deal about Jupiter. It took a year and a half for the two sportscar-size craft to cross the great distance to Jupiter (five times Earth's distance from the Sun). They sent back more than 33,000 photographs of Jupiter and its four large moons. We learned many things about the planet. We also discovered that Jupiter has a great flat ring of dust about one kilometer (0.6 mile) thick. It stretches 58,000 kilometers (36,000 miles) out from the planet.

Jupiter is a planet without a surface. Its dense and deep atmosphere is mostly hydrogen, along with helium and some ammonia, methane, and other gases. From space, all we see are the tops of the hydrogen clouds, pulled into colorful, ever-changing bands by the planet's swift rotation. (Jupiter's day lasts only 10 hours!)

A Voyager spacecraft took this close-up photograph of Jupiter and its two moons, Io and Europa.

The Great Red Spot is a large colorful "storm" of gases that has been visible in Jupiter's clouds for more than 300 years.

The cloud tops at the edge of space are a frigid −130°C. About 1,000 kilometers (620 miles) down, though, the hydrogen is dense enough to form a steamy slush at about 1,000°C. This hydrogen "ocean" may be 20,000 kilometers (12,500 miles) deep. Beneath it, the hydrogen is probably solid and may act like a metal, which would explain Jupiter's powerful magnetic field. Jupiter's core may be an Earth-size ball of iron and rock at 25,000°C.

Jupiter's most striking feature is the Great Red Spot. About twice the size of Earth, it is a high-pressure region of gases that floats near the equator. It changes color from a bright red to a dull brick red and back again.

Life on Jupiter?

Is it possible that simple life forms may exist deep within a warm zone in Jupiter's clouds? Scientists think that certain life-giving chemicals may have formed within the warm clouds. Those chemicals help add color to Jupiter's cloud tops when they are tossed about by strong winds within the clouds. Perhaps simple Jupiter life forms have evolved from those chemicals and live floating among the clouds. Or perhaps Jupiter's violent atmosphere has prevented life forms from evolving. We do not know the answer. But the National Aeronautics and Space Administration (NASA) has plans to send a space probe down through Jupiter's air to find out what is there.

Jupiter's Major Moons

At latest count, Jupiter has 17 moons. Several of them are small bodies that probably are captured asteroids. There are four large moons, discovered by Galileo in 1610. The smallest is the size of our Moon, while the largest is as big as Mercury. They are Io, Europa, Ganymede—the largest moon in the Solar System—and Callisto.

JUPITER'S MAJOR MOONS

NAME	DIAMETER	DISTANCE FROM JUPITER
Ganymede	5,275 km	1 million km
Callisto	4,820 km	2 million km
Io	3,630 km	422,000 km
Europa	3,130 km	670,000 km

Io is the most fascinating moon in the Solar System. Voyager found 10 active volcanoes on Io. The volcanoes throw out enough matter to completely cover over Io's surface once every million years. There are dried lava beds and pools of molten sulfur at 600°C. Io has a frozen crust of sulfur, which may cover a liquid sulfur ocean.

Why is Io so active? The gravity of Jupiter, Europa, and Ganymede tug on Io from opposite directions. This gravitational "tug of war" gives Io a strange orbit. First, Io is pulled in close to Jupiter. Then it is tugged away again by Jupiter's moons. When Io is close, Jupiter's gravity changes Io's shape. When Jupiter is far away, Io's shape changes again. This stretching and squeezing action keeps Io hot inside and keeps its volcanoes active.

Europa is almost the size of our Moon. It has a surface of water ice marked with cracks. The ice is broken into huge plates that may be floating on a sea of liquid water that covers a rock-metal core. The icy surface looks smooth. But it is cobwebbed with dark cracks thousands of kilometers long. The cracks may mark the edges of the ice plates.

Ganymede, king of the moons, is larger than Mercury. Its surface is covered with great plates of water ice that seem to rest atop a thick mantle of ice. Beneath the mantle ice, there may be a solid core of rock. Many craters, some with bright rays, pepper Ganymede's surface. The ice crust also has giant grooves that curve over the surface.

Callisto may have more craters than any other object in the Solar System. Its surface of ice seems to have been bombarded nearly flat by asteroid strikes. The most outstanding marking on Callisto is an ice basin named Valhalla. It is a scar left by a very large asteroid impact. The hole in the center of Valhalla is about 20 kilometers (12 miles) deep and about half as wide as Maine.

SATURN:
The Planet with Ears

Saturn, the Sun's sixth planet, was thought to be the end planet in the Solar System before telescopes were invented. It is the second largest planet, large enough for 800 Earths to fit inside. At a distance twice that of Jupiter from the Sun, it takes Saturn 30 Earth years to orbit the Sun once. Like Jupiter, it rotates rapidly, once every ten and a half hours. To the eye it is a dull-looking object, but telescopes show it as the most beautiful object in the Solar System. One thing that adds to its beauty is its grand system of rings. When Galileo first looked at the planet through his telescope in 1610, he saw the rings as small knobs on either side and he said that Saturn had "ears." Saturn has more moons than any other planet, 22 at latest count.

Speeding along about 50,000 kilometers (31,000 miles) an hour, it took the Voyager spacecraft a little more than three years to reach Saturn. When the Voyagers were about a million kilometers (620,000 miles) from Saturn, they passed into the planet's powerful magnetic field. Saturn's magnetic field is a thousand times stronger than Earth's.

A Trip to Saturn's Center

A view over Saturn's cloud tops would show a pale yellow world enclosed in a thin haze of hydrogen. In Saturn's southern hemisphere clouds is a mysterious reddish oval more than 10,000 kilometers (6,200 miles) long and circled by a dark ring. Maybe it is something

Saturn has thousands of rings and ringlets. A close-up view of the planet shows its colorfully banded atmosphere.

like Jupiter's Great Red Spot. Saturn's clouds are less active than Jupiter's. This may be because of the lower temperatures of Saturn's cloud tops, about −180°C. But strong winds tear at the clouds, blowing at 1,770 kilometers (1,100 miles) an hour. Fierce storms also rage within Saturn's clouds. Some of the storms are larger than Asia.

Saturn's air is mostly hydrogen and helium with some methane and ammonia ice mixed in. About 1,000 kilometers (620 miles) down there may be clouds of water vapor and ammonia, but no one knows for sure. Beneath that there may be an ocean of liquid hydrogen. Saturn's core may be a lump of rock about twice as large as Earth.

Saturn's Rings

When Galileo first gazed on Saturn's rings he did not understand what he saw. Nearly 50 years passed before a Dutch astronomer correctly said that Saturn's "ears" were really rings. The ring system is not one smooth ring but more than 1,000 separate rings. The distance from the inner edge of the rings to the outer edge is more than 70,000 kilometers (45,000 miles). The rings are very thin, from only 9 meters (30 feet) to 150 meters (500 feet) thick. The rings look like a phonograph record.

How Saturn's rings were formed is still a mystery. The ring pieces are lumps of ice mixed with dust. Some are as small as salt grains, others are the size of a railroad boxcar. Some astronomers have wondered if Saturn's rings are the remains of a moon that wandered too close to Saturn and was shattered by the planet's strong gravity. Many astronomers think that the ring pieces are matter that was left over after Saturn was formed.

Before the Voyager fly-bys, scientists wondered what held Saturn's rings together. Why don't they fly apart? The answer seems to be some of the moons of Saturn. The moons' gravity seems to keep the rings "fenced in."

While the Voyagers answered many questions about Saturn, they left unanswered many more. One interesting puzzle is the mysterious lightninglike flashes within the rings.

The Moons of Saturn

At latest count Saturn has 22 moons. The largest one is Titan, the second largest moon in the Solar System after Jupiter's Ganymede. All of Saturn's moons seem to be made of water ice. Some contain rock as well. Voyager sent back photographs showing Saturn's moons peppered with craters. The moon Mimas has a crater nearly one quarter its own size. Some craters of Saturn's moons are

400 kilometers (250 miles) across. There also are deep cracks in the ice. The cracks may have formed when the core regions of the moons froze, expanded, and so cracked the surface ice. The moon Iapetus is something of a mystery. One side of it shines from 10 to 15 times brighter than the other side. The dark side is as dark as tar while the bright side is as light as snow. The dark side may have carbon mixed into the surface ice making it dark.

SATURN'S MAJOR MOONS

NAME	DIAMETER	DISTANCE
Titan	5,140 km	1,221,000 km
Rhea	1,530 km	526,000 km
Dione	1,120 km	387,000 km
Tethys	1,060 km	295,000 km
Enceladus	500 km	238,000 km
Mimas	390 km	187,000 km
Hyperion	300 km	1,481,000 km

Titan is Saturn's most interesting moon, wrapped in a dense atmosphere that glows with a reddish-orange light. It is the only moon in the Solar System with an atmosphere, which is 280 kilometers (175 miles) deep. The moon's air is mostly nitrogen. Its surface is about −185°C and may have large lakes of liquid nitrogen near the poles. Titan seems to be about half water ice and half rock. We can rule out life on Titan since the moon is too cold and lacks liquid water.

Six of Saturn's more than 20 moons are shown in a close-up view. Titan is the only moon in the Solar System with a dense atmosphere.

SATURN

Dione

Mimas

Titan

Rhea

Enceladus

Iapetus

Tethys

URANUS
DIAMETER: 51,800 kilometers
(32,190 miles)
DISTANCE FROM SUN:
2,870,000,000 kilometers
(1,783,000,000 miles)
ROTATION: 13 hours 24 minutes (backward)
REVOLUTION: 84.01 Earth
years
SPEED IN ORBIT: 6.8 kilometers per second (4.2 miles
per second)
GRAVITY: If you weigh 85
pounds on Earth, your
weight on Uranus would be
79 pounds.
MOONS: 15
In Roman mythology, Uranus
was the father of Saturn
and the grandfather of
Jupiter.
A symbol for Uranus is

URANUS: A Tipped-Over Planet

For 2,000 years no one suspected that there were three more planets beyond Saturn—Uranus, Neptune, and Pluto. On the night of March 13, 1781, the English astronomer William Herschel was studying the sky with his telescope. He came to a "star" that he had not examined before. For several nights he watched it and saw that it was gliding backward (from west to east) among the stars. He knew that stars were never seen to move that way. They always seemed to move across the sky as a group, from east to west. So the object must be something else. Also, the object was not a sharp pinpoint of light, as stars appear. Instead it was a small and faint spot. Other astronomers watched this "new" object and soon realized it was not a star at all. Herschel became the first person to discover a planet—Uranus.

Uranus lies twice Saturn's distance from the Sun and is about half Saturn's size. It is a greenish world tipped over on its side. While one pole is bathed in sunlight for 42 Earth years, the other pole has night just as long. In 1986, Voyager 2 discovered that Uranus has ten rings. They are very thin and as dark as coal dust. They may be made up of lumps of dark rock, or they may be glassy matter. Some astronomers say that the rings may be broken pieces of one or more moons.

Uranus's rings are much narrower than Saturn's and they have sharper edges. Seven of the ten rings probably are less than 10 kilometers (6 miles) across. Another may be about 100 kilometers (62 miles) across. From one outer edge to the other, the ring system spans about 100,000 kilometers (62,000 miles). That is only about one-third the width of Saturn's rings.

We know little about Uranus. It seems to be a "gas giant" planet like Saturn and Jupiter. The tops of its clouds are about −215°C and are mostly hydrogen and helium. Like other "gas giants," Uranus probably is made up mostly of hydrogen, with methane, ammonia, helium, and other gases mixed in. It is probably very hot inside and may have layers of hydrogen slush, water and ammonia slush, and possibly a rock-metal core hotter than the surface of the Sun.

At latest count Uranus has 15 moons. They range in size from 300 kilometers (185 miles) across to 1,600 kilometers (990 miles) across. All 15 moons are aligned along the tipped-over equator of Uranus, so they are seen in a line going up and down the sky.

Uranus appears greenish because of certain chemicals, such as methane, in its atmosphere.

NEPTUNE: The Last Giant

Could there be still more planets beyond Uranus? Astronomers living after Herschel wondered. But they had to wait 65 years for the answer. In 1846 a German astronomer at the Berlin Observatory became the first to gaze on Neptune and know that it was a planet.

How to Discover a Planet

The story begins with an English college student named John C. Adams. He became interested in Uranus when he read reports of its "strange motion." As soon as Uranus was discovered, astronomers began to figure out its speed and the path it followed around the Sun. But there was a problem. Sometimes Uranus was ahead of where it should be in its orbit, and other times it was behind where it should be. What could cause Uranus to act that way?

Adams had an idea. Wasn't it true that all objects in space attracted each other by their gravity? Didn't the Sun attract Earth and the other planets and so keep them in orbit? Adams next asked: What if there is a large slow-moving planet out beyond Uranus? Wouldn't that planet's gravity tug at Uranus when Uranus passed that planet as the two orbited the Sun? When Uranus came near the planet, the planet would pull Uranus toward it and so speed it up a bit. At such times Uranus would be a bit ahead of where it should be in its orbit. Then when Uranus had passed the planet, the planet would be tugging on Uranus and so slowing it down a bit. At such times Uranus would be a bit behind where it should be in its orbit.

Neptune's giant moon, Triton, is about to eclipse the Sun in this painting.

Adams worked out where in the sky a planet must be to cause the "strange motion" of Uranus. In 1845, he wrote a letter to England's chief astronomer, Sir George Biddell Airy, and asked him to look in a certain part of the sky for the new "planet." But Airy did nothing about the letter for several months. Perhaps it was because Adams was young and unknown as an astronomer. Finally, Airy asked an astronomer named James Challis to follow Adams's instructions and search for the planet. A month later Challis saw it through his telescope, but he thought it was just another faint star. There the matter rested.

In France, meanwhile, a mathematician named Urbain Leverrier took up the problem. He also worked out the position of the unknown planet. Leverrier wrote a letter to a German astronomer named Johann G. Galle and asked Galle to search a certain part of the sky for the planet. Galle got the letter September 23, 1846. That very night he pointed his telescope where Leverrier had said. There it was, in clear view! The new planet was named Neptune, after the Roman god of the sea.

The Blue Planet

Neptune is so very far away it is hard to see the planet in much detail. It is 30 times Earth's distance from the Sun and appears as a dim bluish-green world through telescopes. Neptune is nearly the same size as Uranus and is thought of as a twin of Uranus. Four Earths could be lined up along Neptune's diameter. Neptune takes 165 Earth years to revolve about the Sun once. But Neptune rotates on its axis faster than Earth. A Neptune day is only 17 hours and 50 minutes long.

The farther out in the Solar System we search with our telescopes, the less we are able to see and learn about objects out there. We can guess that Neptune's core is something like Uranus's. It may be a rock-metal ball about 15 times Earth's mass. Above this core region may be ices of water and ammonia topped by clouds of hydrogen and helium. The clouds are about $-230°C$. Neptune is so far from the Sun that it receives much less heat and light than Venus and Earth do, for example. But the planet's very hot core region— probably $7,000°C$—gives off heat. In fact, Neptune gives off more heat than it receives from the Sun. That is also true of Jupiter. Our telescopes show two, maybe even three, moons orbiting Neptune.

We cannot expect to learn much more about Neptune and its moons through telescopes. To get a close-up view that will show details of the planet we will have to send robot explorers like the two Voyagers to study the planet and its moons. Such a visit may take place when Voyager reaches Neptune—a stop scheduled for 1989.

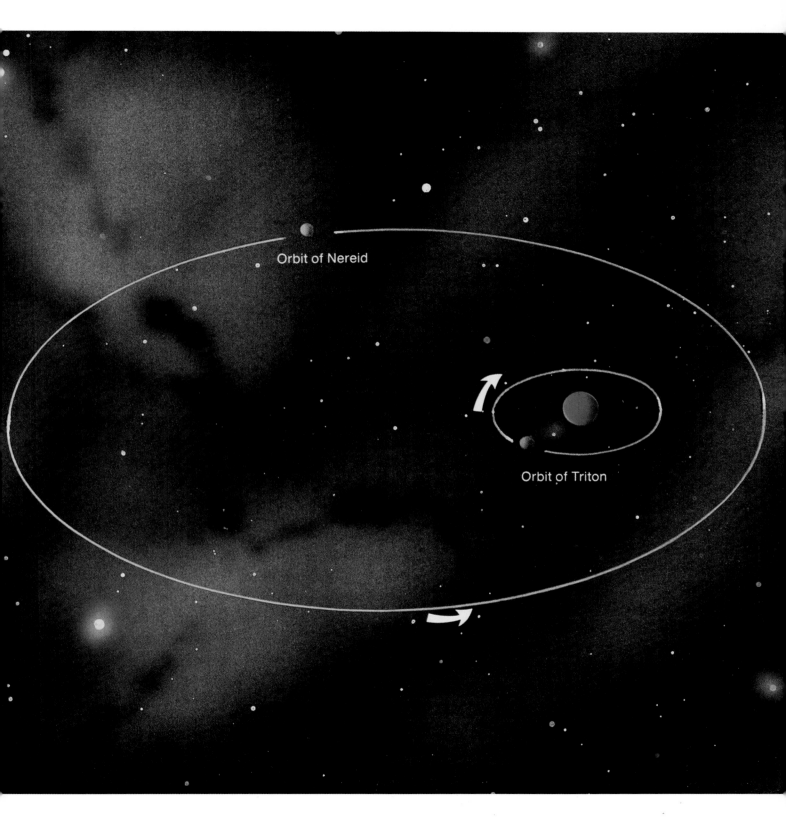

Neireid, the smaller of Neptune's two known moons, orbits Neptune in the same direction as the planet orbits the Sun. Triton, the larger moon, orbits Neptune in the opposite direction — opposite to the direction in which Neptune spins.

PLUTO

DIAMETER: 3,000 kilometers (1,865 miles)

DISTANCE FROM SUN: 5,900,000,000 kilometers (3,666,000,000 miles)

ROTATION: 6 days 9 hours (backward)

REVOLUTION: 248 Earth years

SPEED IN ORBIT: 4.7 kilometers per second (2.9 miles per second)

GRAVITY: If you weigh 85 pounds on Earth, your weight on Pluto would be 2.5 pounds.

MOONS: 1

In Roman mythology, Pluto was the god of the underworld.

A symbol for Pluto is ♇

PLUTO: The Last Planet?

About 40 times Earth's distance from the Sun lies the last known planet in the Solar System. It is the smallest of the planets, smaller even than our Moon. In fact, many astronomers doubt if it is a real planet at all. And Pluto's long and tilted orbit adds to the planet's mystery. .

Not even the strongest telescopes tell us much about Pluto, because it is so far away. We do know that it takes 248 Earth years for Pluto to circle the Sun, and that, unlike the gas giants, it is a small world, probably made of frozen gases. It is certainly the coldest place in the Solar System, because it is so far from the Sun. We also know that Pluto has a moon, named Charon. It was discovered by James Christy in 1978.

Many astronomers think that, properly speaking, Pluto is not a planet at all. For one thing, it follows a long, stretched-out orbit that crosses the orbit of Neptune. So Pluto is sometimes closer to the Sun than Neptune is. From 1979 to 1999, Neptune will be the most distant planet in the Solar System. Pluto's orbit is strange in another way. It is tilted away from the evenly arranged orbits of the other planets.

Pluto is more like one of the moons of the giant planets than like the planets themselves. Some astronomers think that Pluto may be an escaped moon of Neptune. Maybe when the Solar System was young a tenth planet swept in close to Neptune. As it did, the tenth planet's gravity tugged Pluto out of orbit from around Neptune. It then flung Pluto off on a new course that sent Pluto around the Sun in a long, stretched-out orbit. Maybe the tenth planet also chipped a piece off Pluto, and the piece became Charon. If so, then where is the tenth planet now? It also would have been flung into a new orbit by Neptune's gravity. Its new orbit would be something like Pluto's, but one that takes the planet so far away from the Sun that the planet visits the inner region of the Solar System only rarely. There is no evidence that Pluto came to be in just that way. It is only a guess.

Maybe we should look on Pluto and Charon as museum pieces. Perhaps they are chunks of icy matter left over from the time the planets were forming. How many Plutos and Charons are orbiting out there in the dark of the outer Solar System no one can say. Maybe there are many waiting to be discovered by the next generation of Voyager spacecraft.

Pluto, as it might appear from its icy moon, Charon.

THE COMETS:
Dirty Snowballs

Not too long ago people were terrified of comets. Comets were called "terrible stars," "death-bringing stars," and "hairy stars." The "hairy," or tail, part of the comet was thought to be made of poisonous gas that would kill people if Earth passed through the tail. In 1910, and 1986, Halley's Comet came around for its once-every-76-years visits. In 1910, greedy merchants fooled the public and sold them comet pills. The sellers said the pills would save people from the poison tail. Today, we know that comets are not stars at all and that passing through a comet's tail would be as harmless as walking through the fog.

What Are Comets?

One astronomer has said that "a comet is about as close to nothing as something can get." The astronomer Fred L. Whipple calls them "dirty snowballs" because they seem to be nothing more than rock dust wrapped around a spongy ball of ice. The comets' rock dust and ice may be matter left over from the time the Sun and planets formed some 4.6 billion years ago.

The Dutch astronomer Jan H. Oort thinks there may be 100 billion comets making up a huge swarm called the Oort Cloud. This cloud encloses the Solar System like a giant balloon some 5 trillion kilometers (3 trillion miles) from the Sun.

Comet Kohoutek, of 1974, was the first comet photographed from space. In the spring of 1986, five space probes were sent to get close-up views of Comet Halley.

A comet may begin when ice chunks of the Oort Cloud are pulled away by a passing star. The star's gravity flings one or more comets from the Oort Cloud and sends it on a long journey toward the Sun. For hundreds of years the comet is pulled toward the Sun by the Sun's gravity. Its orbit is a long one in the shape of a cigar. Eventually the comet zooms in among the planets. The loose lump of rock dust and ice forming the comet is called the nucleus. It may be from 1 kilometer (0.6 mile) to 100 kilometers (62 miles) across. As the nucleus is heated by the Sun, some of its ice changes into a gas. The gas forms a cloud called the coma. The coma may swell out to a million kilometers (620,000 miles) from the nucleus. At this stage we may see the comet as a fuzzy ball glowing in space.

The comet gets still closer to the Sun. As it does, sunlight and the solar wind push some of the gases of the coma out into a long glowing tail. One of the most beautiful comet tails ever seen was that of the comet named Ikeya-Seki. It was seen in the night sky for months in 1965, and it had a tail 120 million kilometers (75 million miles) long. That is almost Earth's distance from the Sun.

Like the planets, comets orbit the Sun. As a comet sweeps around the Sun and begins its journey away, something interesting happens to its tail. The Sun keeps pushing the tail away from the nucleus. So on its outward journey from the Sun the comet travels tail-first.

Comet Families

Some comets travel back toward the Oort Cloud and take hundreds or thousands of years to return to the Sun again. Because those comets have such long periods of return, they are called long-period comets. Others never make it past the giant planets. Some of these comets are attracted by Jupiter and end up in orbit with Jupiter at one end and the Sun at the other end. Each of the four giant planets has captured comets in that way and has its own comet family. Because those comets return to loop around the Sun every several years, they are called short-period comets. Comet Encke has the shortest period of any comet known. It returns to the Sun once every 3.3 years. Halley's Comet has a period of 76 years. Comets are named after the people who discover them. Halley's Comet was named after the English astronomer Edmund Halley.

Some comets show up right on time. Others may be a bit early or a bit late. Why? When a comet nears the Sun and is heated, gas jets from the nucleus sometimes act as rocket engines and speed up the comet or change its course a bit. Sometimes these gas jets break the nucleus in two, or shatter it. Astronomers know of at least 15 comets where the nucleus has been broken into many pieces. Each time a comet circles the Sun, part of the comet breaks up. Eventually all

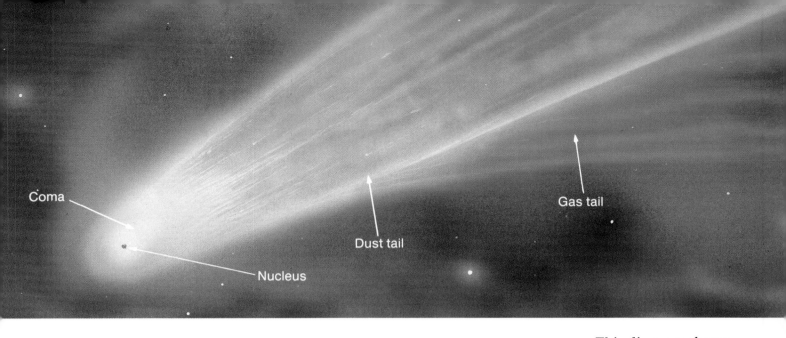

Coma

Gas tail

Dust tail

Nucleus

that may be left of the comet is a long swarm of pieces of matter the size of sand grains and pebbles. Earth sweeps through these swarms from time to time. When it does, the remains rain down on us as streaks of light in the night sky called meteor showers. Meteor showers are named after the group of stars, or constellation, from which they seem to rain. The Orionids shower, for example, was thought by ancient peoples to come from the constellation Orion, the Hunter.

This diagram shows the parts of a comet.

The Oort Cloud is a giant shell of billions of comets that may enclose the Solar System. This is an artist's view.

THE STARS: Flares in the Night

Beyond the far edge of the Solar System lie the stars. And there are billions upon billions of them marching endlessly out of sight. There are red stars, blue-white stars, yellow stars, orange stars, and black stars. Some stars are very much smaller than the Sun, and others are very much larger. There are stars that shine quietly, and there are stars that end their lives in giant explosions. And there are stars that disappear inside themselves as black holes.

Supernova and Nova Stars

On July 4 in the year 1054, Chinese astronomers saw a strange event in the sky. It was a star whose outer layer of gases exploded into space. Such stars are called supernovas. Today we see the remains of that supernova as a bright cloud of gas called the Crab Nebula. After almost 1,000 years, the matter hurled off when the star exploded is still spreading out across space. It is speeding out at 1,300 kilometers (800 miles) a second. When a supernova explodes, the star gets brighter and brighter for about a week. Then it may stay bright for several days or a few months. After that it slowly grows dim over three or four weeks. Another supernova was seen on November 11, 1572, and another in the year 1604. The 1572 supernova was so bright that people saw it during the day. Those three are the only supernovas we know of in our home galaxy. But astronomers have found more than 400 supernovas in galaxies beyond the Milky Way.

The Crab Nebula is a gas cloud that was made by a
supernova explosion and seen in 1054 B.C.

Supernova stars have a lot of matter packed into them—30 or more times as much matter as the Sun has. The temperature at the surface of these massive stars is hundreds of times hotter than the Sun. In only one second a supernova star gives off as much energy as the Sun does in about 60 years.

Stars called nova stars are baby copies of supernova stars. They grow bright over a few days or a few weeks, then they dim and again shine as they did before. On March 10, 1935, a nova star brightened in the constellation Hercules. But by May 6 it had gone back to its usual brightness. Maybe 50 or so nova stars flare up in our galaxy each year.

Planetary Nebulae and Variable Stars

Stars misnamed "planetary nebulae" also explode and hurl matter off into space. The beautiful star shown in the painting on page 62 is in the constellation Aquarius and can be seen through a telescope. It seems to have a ring of matter enclosing it. That star exploded long ago and hurled matter off into space. The ring really is a shell, or a balloon, enclosing the star. It looks like a ring only because the edge around the shell is thicker than the center part. This shell of gas is speeding out in all directions at about 16 kilometers (10 miles) a second. What makes these stars hurl part of themselves off into space is still a mystery.

Some stars flash on and off like fireflies, but much slower. They are called variable stars because their light varies, or changes. Astronomers have found more than 18,000 variable stars in our galaxy. Many belong to a group named after a well-known variable star called Mira, in the constellation Cetus. All variable stars go from dim to bright and then back to dim again. How fast they do this depends on what kind of variable star they are. The Mira variable stars pulse from dim to bright and then back to dim again over a period of about 300 days. During one such period, a Mira-type variable star grows about 15 times brighter than when it is dim. Some variable stars have periods of growing bright and then dim and then bright again lasting from a few days to about 50 days. Others have periods of only 6 to 18 hours.

Giant Stars and Dwarf Stars

There are stars that are several hundred times bigger than the Sun. There are red giant and supergiant stars like the two red stars marking the right shoulder of that great hunter in the sky, the constellation Orion. And there are blue-white giant and supergiant stars, like the brightest star in Orion and like the brightest star in the constellation the Little Dog.

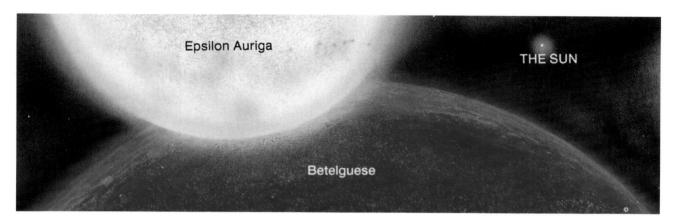

Epsilon Auriga

THE SUN

Betelguese

The surface gases of the red giant stars are only about half as hot (3,000 kelvins) as the Sun's surface gases (6,000 kelvins). So the cooler red giant stars are dimmer than the hotter Sun-like stars. The giant stars may have 10 times or so more matter than a star like the Sun.

There are dwarf stars, too. Most are red dwarfs, and we know of many. Their reddish light means that their surface gases also are cool (about 3,000 kelvins). There also are white dwarf stars. Their white light tells us that the surface gases of these stars are much hotter than the Sun and the red dwarfs. There also are black dwarf stars. These are stars that have stopped shining and have ended their lives.

Can astronomers make any sense out of the different kinds of stars we see in the sky? Is it possible that certain of these stars are like pieces of a puzzle? That if we put them together in just the right way we can learn something about the life story of a star? How a star begins its life, how it shines for a long time, and then how one day it stops shining and goes out?

Red supergiant and giant stars, such as Epsilon Auriga and Betelguese, are hundreds of times larger than the Sun.

A star forms from a cloud of gas and dust.

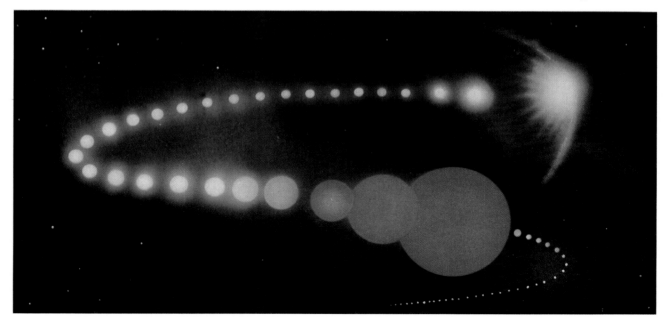

THE STARS: Their Life Stories

Where do stars come from? They have not always been shining as we see them now. And they cannot keep on shining forever. One day each star must go out. What happens to a star when it goes out?

The Birthplace of Stars

Wherever astronomers point their telescopes, they see huge clouds of gas and dust out among the stars of the Milky Way. They also see such clouds of gas and dust in other galaxies. Those clouds are called nebulae. They are mostly hydrogen gas along with some helium.

There are three main kinds of nebulae. A dark nebula is a cold cloud of gas and dust. Because a dark nebula does not shine, we see it outlined by bright stars shining behind the nebula. The Horsehead Nebula is a dark nebula. A reflection nebula is a hot cloud of gas and dust with one or more stars inside it. The cloud shines with the light of those stars—like a firefly blinking in a cloud of fog. Clouds of gas around those stars forming the group called the Pleiades are examples of reflection nebulae. An emission nebula is a very hot cloud of gas and dust that shines with its own light. The Trifid Nebula is a beautiful emission nebula.

The Trifid Nebula gives off colorful light as it shines, much the way a fluorescent light bulb shines.

How Stars Are Born

The nebulae seem to be the birthplace of stars. In many nebulae we have found very dense and dark clouds called globules. A globule grows as its gravity pulls surrounding matter into itself. As the globule keeps getting larger and larger, it becomes a protostar, meaning "early star." The hydrogen and helium matter of the protostar tumble down into the core region. This packing of matter in the core makes the protostar heat up. It keeps heating up until it begins to glow red. In time, the temperature in the core zooms up to about 10 million kelvins. When that happens the core becomes hot enough for the hydrogen to fuse into helium (as you found in the chapter "The Sun: Our Local Star").

If the star is like our Sun it shines with a yellowish-white light. The gases at the surface are about 6,000 kelvins. The gases in the core are about 15 million kelvins. These Sun-like stars shine for about 10 billion years.

If the protostar doesn't have as much matter as the Sun, it doesn't get hot enough to shine with a yellowish-white light. Instead, it shines with a reddish light. Such stars have only about one-tenth as much mass, or matter, as the Sun. They are the red dwarf stars. Their surface temperatures are only about 3,000 kelvins. Their core temperatures never go much above 10 million kelvins. That means

that the red dwarf stars are using up their hydrogen fuel much more slowly than Sun-like stars. Because they do, the red dwarfs have very long lives, perhaps a trillion years or so.

If the protostar has much more matter than the Sun, it gets so hot that it shines with a bluish-white light. Such stars have about 10 to 30 times more mass than the Sun. They are the blue giants and supergiants. Their surface temperatures are about 30,000 kelvins or more. Their core temperatures go up to around 40 million kelvins. These stars use up their hydrogen fuel very fast. They have short lives of only millions of years.

How Stars Die

The smallest red dwarf stars burn so slowly that even one formed in the earliest days of the Universe is still shining now. That is not true of other stars. What is in store for the Sun? Earlier we said that the Sun's life as a star is about 10 billion years long. The Sun is now about 5 billion years old. In another 5 billion years the Sun will begin to go out. But how?

At that time the Sun's hydrogen will be about used up. That means there will be no more hydrogen to fuse into helium in the core region. And that means the core will begin to cool down. As it does,

The Sun was formed from a huge cloud of gas and dust.

the outer layers of the Sun will tumble in toward the core region. That will quickly heat up the core so much that a burst of energy will cause the Sun to swell up into a giant star shining with red light. So the Sun will become a red giant. It will be so big that it will swallow up Mercury and Venus. By that time it will be so hot on Earth that the oceans will boil away and all the surface rocks will melt. All life on Earth will end.

Once again the red giant Sun's core will cool down. And once more the Sun's outer layers will fall in toward the core region. But there will be no more bursts of energy. Instead, the Sun will shrink until it is no bigger than Earth. It will then be so hot that it will shine with a bright white light. It will have become a white dwarf star. For billions of years more the white dwarf Sun will cool. Finally it will become a cold object that no longer shines. It will then be a black dwarf.

The same fate awaits the red dwarf stars. When they also use up their hydrogen fuel they will puff up for a while as red giants and then shrink to white dwarf stars.

What happens to the very massive blue giant and supergiant stars? When they run out of hydrogen the core region cools down a bit. When it does, the outer layers of gases tumble in toward the core so violently that the stars explode as supernova stars. All that is left of a supernova star is the exposed hot core. All the outer layers of gases have been hurled off into space.

A supernova core is only about 16 kilometers (10 miles) across. But it is so tightly packed that a lump of its matter the size of a sugar cube would weigh 10 million tons. In 1967 British astronomers discovered one of these tightly packed stars spinning very fast. Each time it spun around it sent out a burst of radio noise. These fast-spinning radio stars are called pulsars. The bright object in the middle of the Crab Nebula is a pulsar spinning around about 30 times a second.

Black Holes

Stars that have even more matter than pulsars have a strange fate in store. They become black holes. One astronomer has said that a black hole is an object that dug a hole, jumped in, and then pulled the hole in after itself! We do not know for certain that black holes really exist. Some astronomers think they do. Others say no, or maybe.

Imagine a star about 10 times more massive than the Sun. The star uses up its hydrogen fuel, swells up as a red giant, then explodes, leaving a tiny hot core only 60 kilometers (40 miles) across. It is so dense, and its gravity so strong, that nothing can escape from the star, not even its own light. The star disappears from sight, though it is still there. It has become a black hole that gobbles up the gases of other stars that happen to be close by.

Up until now we have found out how astronomers think planets are formed, and how they think stars are born and die. But what about the Universe itself? How did it begin, and how do we think it may end?

This is one artist's view of a black hole.

THE BIG BANG: How It All Began

It was the most fantastic explosion anyone can imagine. What was to become every piece of matter in the Universe was packed into a tiny bit of matter, a super-atom. Sometime between 12 and 20 billion years ago that super-atom exploded in what astronomers call the Big Bang.

At that moment, time and the Universe began. The fireball explosion of the Big Bang sent matter rushing off in all directions. The Universe began to grow larger, or expand, and it has been expanding ever since.

The First Kinds of Matter

At first, nearly all of the Universe was a cloud of hot hydrogen. Some of the hydrogen fused and formed helium, as happens today in the hot cores of stars. But then the hydrogen became too cool for more fusion to take place. Only a few minutes after the Universe was born, nine-tenths of its mass became hydrogen and one-tenth became helium.

The Galaxies Form

By about 100,000 to a million years after the Big Bang, the hydrogen and helium had formed giant clouds. Some parts of space had bigger clouds than other parts. The gravity of these bigger clouds attracted and swallowed up smaller clouds. Gravity also caused the bigger clouds to be packed tighter and tighter. These clouds of hydrogen and helium were the beginnings of the galaxies.

The Big Bang theory is one idea about how the Universe was formed.

Each new galaxy-cloud had smaller cloud clumps of hydrogen and helium. These smaller clouds then became the birthplaces of stars and planets. Today there are billions of galaxies. All of them seem to be 10 billion years old or more.

The Expanding Universe

When we say that the Universe is expanding, we mean that the galaxies are rushing away from each other at great speed. Some astronomers think that the Universe will keep on expanding forever. Others think that it may slow down and stop expanding one day. All the galaxies may then start tumbling back in, drawn by gravity. Billions of years later, they may all smash together and form another super-atom that will explode in another Big Bang. These astronomers think that the cycle of expansion and explosion may never end.

No one knows for certain how the Universe began. Maybe it always has existed—without a beginning or an end. We can study the stars through telescopes, make measurements, make guesses, send robot spacecraft to the planets or visit them ourselves. But scientists will never know all there is to know about the Universe. Science is an endless search for knowledge. Each new discovery scientists make about a planet, a star, or a galaxy makes us a little bit richer in our knowledge about the world.

What will future probes of the Universe discover?

GLOSSARY

Asteroids   Chunks of rock and metal circling the Sun in orbits between Mars and Jupiter. The asteroid belt probably is the source of most meteoroids.

Big Bang   The idea that the Universe began with the explosion of a tiny but tightly packed bit of matter that contained all the matter the Universe was ever to have.

Black Hole   A tightly packed star that is so dense its strong gravity lets nothing escape from the star, not even light.

Comet   Member of the Solar System that orbits the Sun. Comets come from far beyond Pluto and seem to be rock dust mixed in a spongy ball of ice.

Crust   The outer layer of solid rock of a planet.

Exosphere   The top layer of Earth's air. Its base starts about 500 kilometers (310) miles above the ground.

Fusion   The act of coming together in a special way is called *fusion*. For example hydrogen atoms in the core of the Sun smash into each other so hard that they join, or *fuse*, and build up into helium atoms.

Galaxy   A collection of billions and billions of stars. Our galaxy is the Milky Way. The Universe has billions of galaxies.

Gravity   The force of any object that pulls other objects toward it. The more mass an object has, the stronger its force of gravity. On a star or planet, gravity pulls objects toward the center.

Ionosphere   An electrically charged layer in Earth's air. The ionosphere reflects radio signals back to Earth.

Kelvin Scale   A temperature scale used by astronomers. Room temperature (68°F) is about 300 on the Kelvin thermometer.

Magnetic Field   The region around a magnet in which magnetic force is present.

Mantle   The layer of melted rock between a planet's core and its crust, or surface rock.

Mass   The amount of matter an object is made of. A large person's body has more mass than a small person's, just as Earth has more mass than the Moon.

Mesosphere   The layer of Earth's air just below the thermosphere. The mesosphere begins about 50 kilometers (30 miles) above the ground and goes up to a height of about 80 kilometers (50 miles).

Meteor   The streak of light caused when a meteoroid speeds through Earth's atmosphere and burns up.

Meteorite   A meteoroid entering Earth's atmosphere from space and surviving the trip to the ground without burning up.

Meteoroid   Any piece of rock or metal most likely resulting from asteroids smashing into each other and breaking into smaller pieces.

Nebula   A huge cloud of gas and space dust out among the stars.

Nova   A star that grows brighter over a few days or a few weeks, then dims and shines as before.

Oort Cloud   A huge swarm of comet bodies enclosing the Solar System like a giant balloon.

Pulsar   A fast-spinning and especially dense star that sends out radio pulses.

Revolution   The motion of one object around another, such as the Moon's motion around Earth, and Earth's motion around the Sun. All the planets in our solar system revolve around the Sun.

Rotation   The motion of a body around its axis, like a spinning top. The Sun and all the planets rotate. Earth rotates once on its axis every 24 hours.

Solar System   The Sun, its nine known planets, more than 45 moons, and meteoroids, asteroids, and comets. The Solar System is one of many planetary systems in the Universe.

Solar Wind   Streams of bits and pieces of atoms hurled off by the Sun. The solar wind "blows" across the Solar System.

Star   A huge sphere, or ball, of hot gases that gives off large amounts of heat, light, and other energy. There are more than 300 billion stars in our galaxy. And there are countless billions more beyond our galaxy.

Stratosphere   The layer of Earth's air starting about 10 kilometers (6 miles) above the ground and going up to a height of about 50 kilometers (30 miles).

Supernova   A massive star that explodes and blows off its outer gas layers, leaving only the exposed core.

Thermosphere   The layer of Earth's air beneath the exosphere. The thermosphere begins 80 kilometers (50 miles) up and stops 500 kilometers (310 miles) up.

Troposphere   Earth's bottom layer of air, where all weather takes place. The troposphere starts at the ground and goes up to a height of about 10 kilometers (6 miles).

INDEX